Heart H

Diet

By

Kay Hersom

Hersom House Publishing

Ocala, Florida

Five Star Reviews!

*"**Wonderful place to start for your heart & Delicious Recipes!** -I'm always looking for new and interesting recipes to be heart healthy. This was a delightful surprise as it contains some very good information for heart awareness. I definitely enjoyed the read. The recipes are not your standard bland heart recipes. There is delicious flavor in those pages! Thank you to the author for the contribution; it may just save another life. Excellent book!"*

*"**You Won't Feel Deprived** - I have a family history of heart disease so I am very conscious of the fact that I'm at risk too. I also want to keep my family healthy. This book pointed out some things to avoid but most of all some awesome recipes. Even dessert. If you use these recipes no one will know they're eating Heart Smart. Simple elegant dishes ....love it.!"*

*"**Choosing Life** - Sorry to hear about what happened to your husband but it seems that you are very conscious of the correct steps to take to make sure that it doesn't happen again. I wish more people could read this book. Sometimes we don't realize until it is too late. Your book has helped me to take a second look at my diet to see if I can incorporate some of the changes you mentioned."*

Heart Healthy Diet

By Kay Hersom

First Published, 2013

Printed in the United States of America

Hersom House Publishing

3365 NE 45th St, Suite 101

Ocala, Florida 34479

This eBook is intentionally published on the Amazon Kindle platform so that you can enjoy it in quick snippets on any mobile device, while in the grocery store, or planning a meal. A Kindle eReader device is not required to enjoy this book; simply download the Kindle App to any Smartphone or mobile device you own to enjoy your Kindle library on the go!

Notice

This book is intended as a reference volume only, not as a medical manual. The information given here is designed to help you make informed decisions about your health. It is not intended as a substitute for any treatment that may have been prescribed by your doctor. If you suspect that you have a medical problem, I urge you to seek competent medical help. As when starting any exercise or diet program consult your doctor before beginning.

Introduction

Last fall my 49 year old husband had a massive heart attack. One of the main arteries in the right part of his heart was 100% blocked. After swift action by a team of Cardiologists and the Grace of God, he recovered. This occurrence sent me into an obsessive mode of spending hours researching everything I could find relating to cardiovascular disease and a heart healthy diet. The amount of information available was exuberant and I felt very overwhelmed. All I needed was a starting point, what can I cook for him? What can we eat if we go out?

So, anyone else who has endured a similar experience, I hope the short version that I have written provides you with basic knowledge, and recipes that you can build upon to enjoy simple and delicious, heart healthy meals... without the frustration.

How to Have a Heart Healthy Diet

Heart disease is the number one killer among men and women in the U.S. and other western countries. Aside from genetics as one of the major factors of heart disease, the food you eat also plays a huge role in the risk of developing it. What you put in your body directly affects your health, and more specifically your heart. Having a heart healthy diet is one way to lower your risk of heart disease, or help you prevent other heart complications. Learning about foods that are bad for your heart is vital to your future health.

Healthy is *being heart smart*.

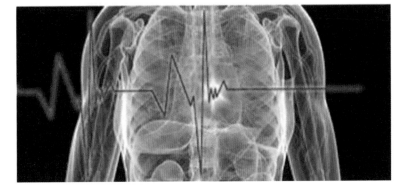

Here Are Foods to Avoid, Foods to Eat, and a Sample of a Heart Healthy Menu

Step One

Avoid foods that are high in fat. Saturated fats and trans-fats should be reduced or even eliminated from your diet. These fats increase the level of your LDL or bad cholesterol, which increases the triglyceride levels in your blood. High triglyceride levels are bad for your heart because they immediately increase after you eat, which can cause high blood pressure, lead to plaque buildup in your arteries, and atherosclerosis, a condition that can limit blood flow to your brain, heart and other parts of your body.

Foods that come from animals such as butter, milk, cheese, meat, among others, have saturated fats. Some plant based foods also contain this fat, like coconut, coconut oil, palm oil and cocoa butter. Trans- fat is the most dangerous fat for your heart. Avoid trans-fats as much as possible since they increase your bad cholesterol and lower your good cholesterol. Foods like, margarine, shortening, packaged and some frozen foods, baked goods, chips, crackers, even some soups, contain trans-fats.

You should also reduce or avoid sugar and sodium. Sugar is turned into glucose in your bloodstream, which then turns into energy. This energy can strain your heart, so monitor your intake of sugar, which comes in soda drinks and many packaged foods. Sodium or salt increases blood pressure, and most processed and fast foods contain a lot of sodium.

Your intake of alcohol should also be monitored. While 2-3 glasses of red wine a day is good for your heart for their antioxidants, excessive consumption can lead to high blood pressure, so avoid beers and hard liquors. If you must drink alcohol, stick to red wine.

Examples of some of the foods that should be avoided are: fried chicken, pork sausages, cheesecakes, steaks, burgers, pizza, French fries, non-whole wheat pasta, dairy based ice cream, doughnuts, and white bread. Knowing what not to eat can drastically improve the health of your heart.

Step Two

Once you reduce and/or eliminate foods that have saturated and trans-fats from your diet, the next step is to know what foods are good for your heart.

Foods rich in Vitamins B-complex, C and E include raw fruits, berries and vegetables and are nutritionally sound foods. Increase your intake of these type foods and incorporate them in every meal. Avoid adding cream, salt, and sugar and avoid canned fruit. Eat them as raw and as fresh as possible. A diet of salmon served together with papaya salsa, pineapples, tomatoes and oranges are all foods rich in vitamins. For breakfast, heart healthy meals may comprise of bran cereal topped with blueberries, or a ripe cantaloupe, and for lunch and dinner, an acorn squash, carrots or sweet potatoes which can be served with tea that is also rich in flavonoids and catechins which are heart protective substances.

Foods like oatmeal, almonds, walnuts, brown rice, whole grains, spinach, kale, broccoli and asparagus are all rich in fiber and are important in maintaining safe cholesterol levels. "An apple (with skin on) a day keeps the doctor away." This old saying could hardly ring more true. Eating legumes is very heart smart and also provides protein in your diet, eliminating meal plans that include red meat. Consuming black beans is not only rich in protein and fiber; they contain magnesium, folate, and antioxidants.

You can also replace red meat with fish. Fish contains healthy fats like omega-3 fatty acids, a polyunsaturated fat, which reduces the chances of experiencing cardiovascular disease. It also helps reduce blood pressure and inflammation. Cold water fish are the best, like salmon, halibut, tuna and herring. Other foods to include in your daily plan that are rich in this nutrient are flack seeds (ground), soybeans, sardines, and tofu. The importance of omega-3 fatty acids in health promotion and disease prevention cannot be overstated.

Olive oil should be used when frying is desired although; grilling and baking/broiling is a healthier way to prepare food.

Step Three

Once you know the foods to eat and the foods to avoid, you now have to know that you should also control the portion of your food. A helpful tool may be to purchase smaller plates and refrain from going back for seconds.

Here is a daily sample of a heart healthy menu:

For breakfast, eat one cup of oatmeal flavored with cinnamon and raisins, along with a cup of coffee.

For lunch, enjoy a low-sodium turkey and tomato sandwich on wheat bread, two cups of fresh spinach leafed salad sprinkled with almonds, and a glass of skim milk.

 For dinner, make grilled salmon with brown rice, steamed broccoli and cauliflower on the side, and a glass of iced tea or red wine.

Though changing your eating habits can be challenging at first, once you get used to eating in a heart healthy way, your body will love you!

Tip: Healthy living has been brought to the forefront over the last several years and many restaurants and food product makers have engaged this wave by offering heart healthy choices. Look for heart healthy labeling on food items in the grocery store and restaurant menus.

Grocery Shopping Helper

The following is a list I put together to help me during the visits to the grocery store. This is by no means a full or compressive list but simply a guide and reminder of what foods I should be thinking of when planning our meals.

Produce

- Fresh Fruit - the more variety the better, mix up the colors

- Fresh Fruit - the more variety the better, mix up the colors

Fish –Frozen and/or Fresh

- Non-breaded fillets

- Non-breaded shellfish

Meats

- Turkey
- Turkey Bacon
- Turkey Sausage
- Lean low-sodium turkey or chicken sandwich meat
- Skinless chicken
- Lean cuts of beef
- Lean hamburger 90/10

Canned & Dried Food

- Fruits canned in juice, not in syrup
- Vegetables low-sodium, and fat-free when available
- Soups low sodium, low-fat
- Canned chicken, low-sodium
- Canned fish, tuna and/or salmon
- Whole grain breakfast cereal
- Oatmeal

- Whole wheat pasta

- Brown rice

- Wild rice

- Whole wheat and whole grain breads

- Whole wheat flour

- Pasta sauce

- Peanut Butter

- Olive Oil

- Canola Oil

- Balsamic Vinegar

- Cooking Sprays

- Salt substitute

Snacks

- Nuts - peanuts, almonds, etc

- Dried fruit - raisins, dates, cranberries, etc

- Popcorn low sodium, low-fat (light)

- Baked potato chips low-sodium

- Seeds, sunflower or flax

- Whole wheat/grain crackers low-sodium

Recipes - Heart Healthy

To get you started, I've included some of my favorite, easy to prepare, heart healthy recipes that taste great!

Starters

Black Bean Dip

Ingredients

- 1 can of refried black beans (fat free)

- 1 tablespoon minced garlic

- 2 tablespoons olive oil

- ½ teaspoon ground cumin

- ½ teaspoon cayenne pepper (optional)

- 1 teaspoon lime juice

- ¼ cup grated cheddar cheese

Preparation

Mix in a blender or food processor all the ingredients except the cheese and blend until smooth. Sprinkle grated cheese on top of the dip when serving. Serve with your favorite tortilla chips, crackers, or pita triangles. May be served at room temperature or warmed up.

Garlic Shrimp

Ingredients

- 1 pound shrimp peeled and deveined

- 2 tablespoons extra virgin olive oil

- 2 tablespoons minced fresh garlic

- ½ red bell pepper chopped

- 2 green onions chopped

- 1 teaspoon hot pepper flakes (optional)

Preparation

In a large skillet add the olive oil and red pepper, at medium heat sauté the red pepper for five minutes. Then add the green onion, garlic and hot pepper flakes (optional depending on your heat level) and continue to sauté until the garlic just starts to turn a golden color. Then add the shrimp and continue to cook until the shrimp are a pinkish color and the garlic is a dark golden color and crisp.

Remove from the heat and serve. To make a salad, serve over salad greens. Additionally you could serve it with pasta or rice to make a meal.

Spicy Sesame Hummus

Ingredients

- 1 can chickpeas drained and rinsed

- ½ cup sesame paste

- 1 tablespoon fresh minced garlic

- 1 tablespoon olive oil

- ½ lemon squeezed for juice

- 1 teaspoon cayenne red pepper (or to personal taste)

Preparation

Combine all ingredients into a food processer and blend until smooth. Serve with pita wedges, crackers, vegetables for dipping or taco chips.

Provolone Topped Portobello with Balsamic Vinegar

Ingredients

- 4 Portobello mushrooms cleaned and stemmed

- 1/2 cup balsamic vinegar

- 1 tablespoon brown sugar or 1 packet of artificial sweetener

- 1/8 teaspoon dried rosemary

- 1 teaspoon minced garlic

- 1/4 cup grated provolone cheese

Preparation

Preheat the oven broiler to 425 degrees. Coat a glass baking dish with cooking spray. Place the mushrooms in the dish bottom side up.

In a bowl mix the vinegar, brown sugar or artificial sweetener, rosemary and garlic. Add mushrooms to the mixture and set aside for 10 minutes to marinate.

Broil the mushrooms, turning once, until they're tender, about 4 minutes on each side. Sprinkle grated cheese over each mushroom and continue to broil until the cheese melts. Serve immediately.

Meals

Grilled Shrimp and Mango Salad

Ingredients

- 2 mangoes, peeled and shredded

- 2 green onions thinly sliced

- 1/3 cup lime juice

- 2 tablespoons fish sauce, or use low sodium soy sauce

- 1 teaspoon sugar

- 1 tablespoon of fresh minced garlic

- 1 serrano pepper, seeded, minced

- 1 pound medium shrimp

- 2 cups salad greens

- lime slices, for garnish

Preparation

Mix green onions, lime juice, fish sauce, sugar, garlic, and pepper in a bowl. Combine shredded mango. Chill while preparing shrimp.

Shell and devein shrimp and divide into 4 portions. Thread each portion onto a slender metal skewer. Grill shrimp on a medium hot grill, covered, for about 3 minutes on each side, or until opaque but still a bit moist in the center of thickest parts.

Place salad greens on a platter; mound mango mixture onto the greens using a slotted spoon. Slide shrimp off skewers and place over the mango salad and garnish with lime slices.

Serves 4

Chicken or Turkey Chili with White Beans

Ingredients

- 2 tablespoons canola oil
- 1 medium onion chopped
- 2 tablespoons fresh minced garlic
- 2 cans Cannellini beans also known as white kidney
- 1 can chicken broth, low-sodium & fat-free 14.5 oz
- 1 can tomatillos drained and chopped 18oz
- 1 can diced tomatoes 16oz
- 1 can sweet corn 16oz
- 1 can diced green chilies 7oz
- ½ teaspoon dried oregano

- ½ teaspoon ground coriander
- ¼ teaspoon ground cumin
- ¼ teaspoon cayenne pepper (optional)
- 1 pound chicken or turkey diced and cooked
- Salt & pepper to taste

Preparation

Heat oil in soup pan, then sauté garlic and onion until soft.

Mix in broth, tomatoes, chilies, tomatillos and spices. Then bring to a boil. Then lower heat to simmer for 10 minutes.

Mix in beans, corn and meat, season with salt and pepper to taste and simmer for 5 additional minutes.

Clam Fettuccine

Ingredients

- 1 - 16oz package fettuccine pasta

- 2 tablespoons minced garlic

- 2 large tomatoes, seeded and chopped

- 2 cups frozen corn

- 1/2 cup chardonnay wine

- 1 tablespoon olive oil

- 4 tablespoons chopped fresh basil

- 2 dozen clams in shell or 2 cans (4 ounces each) clams, drained

- 1/4 teaspoon salt

- Ground black pepper, to taste

Preparation

Cook the pasta according to the package preparation. Drain the pasta thoroughly.

In a large saucepan, add the garlic, tomatoes, corn, wine, olive oil and basil. Cover and bring to a boil for 3-5 minutes, stirring frequently. Reduce heat to lowest setting and add the clams and pasta. Toss gently to coat. Season with salt and pepper and it's ready to serve.

Seared Tuna Steak Crusted with Black & White Sesame with Asparagus Spears

Ingredients

- 4 Tuna Steaks

- 4 Tablespoons olive oil or canola oil

- ½ cup white sesame seed

- ¼ cup black sesame seed

- Sea salt & course ground black pepper to taste

- Garlic powder to taste

- Cayenne pepper to taste (optional)

- 1 pound asparagus spears

Preparation

Asparagus

Roll asparagus spears in oil and then season with sea salt and garlic powder. Place flat on a cookie sheet. Using aluminum foil to cover the cookie sheet works well for easy clean up.

Place under oven broiler set at 425 degrees and cook until just slight browning appears and then take out and turn spears and cook for one more minute.

Tuna

In a bowl mix the black & white sesame seeds. Season the tuna with your desired combination and roll in the sesame seeds coating the tuna. Use a non stick pan and warm the oil until smoking then place the tuna steaks in the pan and cook until the white sesame seeds start to turn golden, approximately one minute. Flip the tuna over and cook around another minute. Move the tuna steaks to a cutting board and cut into 1/4 inch thick slices and serve with a side of asparagus spears.

Eggplant Parmesan

Ingredients

- 2 medium sized eggplants cut crosswise into rounds about 1/3 inch each.

- 2 1/4 teaspoons salt

- 1 Jar of spaghetti sauce 24 oz

- 1 1/2 cups olive oil

- 20 fresh basil leaves torn in half

- 3/4 teaspoon black pepper

- 1/4 teaspoon cayenne pepper (optional)

- 1 cup all-purpose flour

- 5 eggs

- 3 1/2 cup panko Japanese bread crumbs

- 2/3 cup of parmesan cheese finely grated

- 1 lb chilled fresh mozzarella cheese thinly sliced

Preparation

Toss eggplant with 2 teaspoons salt in a colander set over a bowl, then let drain 30 minutes. Preheat oven to 375°F. Mix together flour, 1/4 teaspoon salt, and 1/4 teaspoon pepper in a shallow dish. Beat eggs in a bowl, then stir together panko and 1/3 cup parmesan cheese in a third dish. Doing one slice at a time cover eggplant in flour, shaking off excess, then dip in egg mixer letting excess drip off, and cover in panko until coated. Place the eggplant slices onto sheets of wax paper arranging slices in one layer.

Heat remaining 1 1/2 cups oil in a deep 12-inch nonstick skillet over moderately high heat until hot, then fry eggplant slices turning over once until golden brown 5 to 6 minutes. Then let drain onto paper towels.

Pour 1 cup tomato sauce in bottom of a rectangular 3 1/2-quart 12 x 12 baking dish and spread evenly. Place about one third of eggplant slices in one layer over sauce overlapping slightly if necessary. Cover eggplant with about one third of remaining sauce and one third of mozzarella. Continue layering with remaining eggplant, sauce, and mozzarella. Sprinkle top with remaining 1/3 cup parmesan cheese. Bake uncovered until cheese is melted and golden, and the sauce is bubbling approximately 35 to 40 minutes.

Cajun Black-eyed Peas

Ingredients

- 3 cups water

- 2 cups dried black-eyed peas

- 1 teaspoon low-sodium chicken-flavored bouillon granules

- 1 15oz can unsalted crushed tomatoes

- 1 large onion finely chopped

- 2 celery stalks finely chopped

- 3 teaspoons minced garlic

- 1/2 teaspoon dry mustard

- 1/4 teaspoon ground ginger

- 1/4 teaspoon cayenne pepper

- 1 bay leaf

Preparation

In a medium saucepan over high heat add 2 cups of the water and black-eyed peas. Bring to a boil for 2 minutes then cover and remove from heat, let stand for 1 hour.

Drain the water leaving the peas in the saucepan. Add the remaining 1 cup of water with the remaining ingredients. Stir together and bring to a boil. Cover and reduce heat to a simmer and cook for 2 hours, stirring occasionally. Add water as necessary to keep the peas covered with liquid. Remove the bay leaf, then can be served as is or over cooked white rice.

Spicy Oh My Cod

Ingredients

- 4 cod fillets about 6ounces each

- 1 tablespoon olive oil

- ½ medium red onion sliced

- 1 lemon juiced

- 1 teaspoon dried parsley

- 1 teaspoon cinnamon

- 1 tablespoon fresh minced garlic

- 1 tablespoon ground cumin

- ¼ teaspoon sea salt

- Dash black pepper

- Dash red cayenne pepper

Preparation

Preheat oven to 400 degrees. Using a cookie sheet, place a 12 x 12 sheet of aluminum foil, spray foil with cooking spray and place cod fillets on the foil. In a bowl mix the remaining ingredients, except the red onion slices. Spread mixture over the fillets and cover with onion slices.

Now cover foil with another sheet of foil and roll up the edges to enclose the fish in a foil packet. Place cookie sheet into oven and bake for 45 minutes, fish should be flakey when done.

Serve with pasta seasoned with olive oil, dried parsley, garlic powder and salt to taste. Optionally you may serve with rice, couscous or salad greens.

Broiled Tomatoes with Mozzarella

Ingredients

- 6 tomatoes

- 1 pound fresh mozzarella cheese

- 2 tablespoons olive oil

- ¼ cup Panko breadcrumbs

- 2 tablespoons fresh basil chopped

- Salt to taste

Preparation

Slice the tomatoes lengthwise into ½ inch thick slices. Using a cookie sheet, spray with olive oil cooking spray. Lay sliced tomatoes on cookie sheet, cover with Panko breadcrumbs, then place slices of mozzarella cheese on top of breadcrumbs, slices should be about ¼ inch thick. Place into oven and set to broil. Cook until cheese is golden.

Remove from oven and sprinkle on top with fresh chopped basil and serve, makes for a great side dish or stand alone meal.

Grilled Salmon with Fresh Herbs

Ingredients

- 3 tablespoons chopped fresh basil

- 1 tablespoon chopped fresh parsley

- 1 tablespoon minced garlic

- 2 tablespoons lemon juice

- 4 salmon fillets

- Cracked black pepper, to taste

- 4 green olives, chopped

- 4 thin slices lemon

Preparation

Salmon may be prepared on an outdoor grill or inside oven broiler. Preheat either one. Coat the grill rack or broiler pan with cooking spray. In a bowl combine the basil, parsley, minced garlic and lemon juice. Spray the fish with cooking spray. Sprinkle with black pepper. Top each fillet with equal amounts of the basil-garlic mixture.

Place the fish herb-side down on the grill, side up for the oven broiler. Cook over high heat. When the edges turn white in about 3 to 4 minutes, turn the fish over and place on aluminum foil. Move the fish to a cooler part of the grill or reduce the heat. Cook until the fish is opaque throughout when tested with the tip of a knife. Remove salmon and garnish plates with green olives and lemon slices.

Desserts

Peach Crisp

Ingredients

- 8 fresh peaches, peeled, pitted and sliced

- 1 tablespoon lemon juice

- 1/3 teaspoon ground cinnamon

- 1/4 teaspoon ground nutmeg

- 1/2 cup whole-wheat flour

- 1/4 cup brown sugar

- 2 tablespoons trans-free margarine, cut into thin slices

- 1/4 cup quick oats

Preparation

Preheat the oven to 375 F. Lightly coat a 9-inch pie pan with cooking spray.

Arrange peach slices in the pie pan. Sprinkle with lemon juice, cinnamon and nutmeg.

In a bowl mix together flour and brown sugar. Using your hands crumble the margarine into the flour and sugar mixture. Add the oats and mix evenly. Sprinkle the flour mixture on top of the peaches.

Bake until peaches are soft and the topping is browned around 30 minutes, best served warm.

Bananas with Rum Raisin Sauce

Ingredients

- 1 tablespoon butter

- 1 tablespoon canola oil

- 1 tablespoon honey

- 2 tablespoons brown sugar

- 3 tablespoons low-fat milk

- 1 tablespoon raisins

- 4 bananas

- 2 tablespoons dark rum or apple cider

Preparation

In a small saucepan melt the butter over medium heat. Whisk in canola oil, honey and brown sugar. Stir continuously until brown sugar is dissolved. Stir in milk a little at a time and then cook until the sauce thickens a bit, stir continuously. Remove from the heat and stir in the raisins. Set aside and keep warm.

Peel the bananas, and then cut each crosswise into 3 sections. Cut each section in half lengthwise. Lightly coat a large nonstick frying pan with the canola oil and place over medium-high heat. Add bananas and sauté until they begin to brown. Transfer to a plate.

Add the rum to the pan, bring to a boil and deglaze the pan, stirring constantly cook until rum is reduced by half, approximately 30 to 45 seconds. Return the bananas to the pan to reheat.

Place bananas on serving dishes and drizzle with the warm sauce and serve immediately.

Poached Pears

Ingredients

- 1 cup orange juice

- 1/4 cup apple juice

- 1 teaspoon ground cinnamon

- 1 teaspoon ground nutmeg

- 4 whole pears

- 1/2 cup fresh raspberries

- 4 fresh mint leaves

Preparation

In a bowl combine the juices, cinnamon and nutmeg. Stir to mix evenly.

Peel the pears and leave the stems. Remove the core from the bottom of the pear. Place in a shallow pan. Add the juice mixture to the pan and set over medium heat. Simmer for about 30 minutes turning pears frequently. Don't boil.

Transfer the pears to individual serving plates. Garnish with raspberries and mint leaves, serve while warm.

Enjoy the Healthy Heart Lifestyle

Remember, staying heart healthy doesn't mean you have to give up all the good things to eat. My wish is that you and your loved ones enjoy a long and prosperous life!

God Bless,

Kay Hersom

More Healthy Eating Tips

Kay Hersom has also written Diabetic Diet Plan which is a great complementary book for the Heart Healthy Diet, and is loaded with additional information that goes "hand in glove" with eating heart smart.

Diabetic Diet Plan

Enjoyed the Book?

Thank you for buying this book. I was hoping you could help your fellow book enthusiasts out and when you have a free second leave you honest feedback about this book on Amazon.com. I certainly want to thank you in advance for doing this.

Printed in Great Britain
by Amazon